I0762399

VERANDA
AMERICAN STYLE
TIMELESS INTERIOR DESIGN
HEARST HOME

VERANDA
AMERICAN STYLE
TIMELESS INTERIOR DESIGN
Susan Hall Mahon
FOREWORD BY
Steele Thomas Marcoux
HEARST HOME

Contents

CHAPTER 1

HALLS OF HISTORY 9

CHAPTER 2

ROOM TO ROAM 33

CHAPTER 3

AMERICAN GLAMOUR 65

CHAPTER 4

BY THE SEA 103

CHAPTER 5

NEW TRADITIONS 127

CHAPTER 6

MODERN VISIONS 149

FOREWORD 7
INDEX 170
PHOTO CREDITS 175

◇◇◇

LEFT The paneled entry of a Mark D. Sikes-designed foyer in Sun Valley, Idaho, accessed via a charming Dutch door, is painted in four different Farrow & Ball shades—two red and two blue—for a warm and outgoing effect.

PAGE 1 On the Dallas terrace of a vivacious home designed by Miles Redd and David Kaihoi, iron furniture with generous tufted cushions outfitted in soft green Stroheim fabric are at one with the surrounding foliage.

PAGES 2-3 Designer Meg Braff and architect Gerard Beekman joined two Nantucket townhomes into a singular escape, crafting a grand living room that communes with the harbor view and graciously seats a crowd among its blue and cream color scheme.

Foreword

As Americans, we spend an awful lot of time reflecting on who we are and what makes us unique. This can seem rather backward-looking, a tedious exercise in the study of our history (just ask any student). But a close examination of our past reminds us that America was born from a desire for change—for something new, something original.

In a nod to the 250th anniversary of the founding of the United States, *VERANDA American Style* is a comprehensive look at our country's most exquisite homes. Exploring the characteristics that define American style remains as challenging—and exciting—as ever. Thanks to the wide variety of regional vernaculars and personal histories, our approach to design and decoration follows no formula. But if there is one thing consistent across our mountains, plains, farms, coasts, and cities, perhaps it is our compulsion to honor the past beautifully while fearlessly embracing the new.

In the chapters that follow, you'll find that duality in the way these designers have approached color and finishes; architecture, light, and space; and materials and artwork. Showcased here, their work is the next chapter of our story, rooted in tradition yet infused with an imaginative and pioneering spirit. I invite you to celebrate our uniquely American style.

STEELE THOMAS MARCOUX

◇◇◇

LEFT A Chicago mudroom hall designed by Summer Thornton is ensconced in a lush vine leaf-patterned wallpaper, above which a trio of ivory pendant lanterns presides. A Michael-Cleary mirror wrapped in leaves and berries augments the verdurous space.

CHAPTER 1

Halls of History

There is a certain allure to things that last. Structures that stand the test of time, furniture forged from earth-born materials and shaped by hand. Colors, patterns, and textures woven together years ago that spark admiration decades later. Such quality—of construction and style—is clear in the trio of American homes featured in this chapter. These abodes of a certain age have witnessed centuries of history, but their new chapters were written by architects, designers, and builders who believe in the power of the past and the importance of carrying it forward with thoughtful, considered restoration.

The iconic designer Sister Parish once said, "Innovation is often the ability to reach into the past and bring back what is good, what is beautiful, what is useful, what is lasting." Whether through a revived historic residence or a new build rife with heritage details, informing our present and future with lessons from the past is always a winning formula in design (and beyond).

Behind the enchantment of restored older homes is the serious undertaking of preservation and revitalization. Designers examine the styles, methods, and materials of the original building's era while adhering to current building codes; they infuse modern conveniences while respecting original character; and in the best of circumstances, they delight in the process and deepen their talents in return. As designer Heather Chadduck Hillegas says of the circa-1695 Williamsburg, Virginia, cottage she updated, "These houses teach us so much about design."

◇◇◇

LEFT A flourish of pattern and ornamental touches fill the sun-drenched landing of a historic hilltop home in Greenwich, Connecticut, designed by Markham Roberts. Taffeta curtains and painted Georgian-style plant stands frame an English Aesthetic Movement chair.

VICTORIAN REVIVAL

Designer Markham Roberts exhibits his playbook for rehabbing historic homes by preserving an early-19th-century Queen Anne and refreshing it for a modern family.

PAGES 10-11 One of Markham's rules for renovating old houses is: "You don't have to stick to the rigidity of a period." He anchored the living room with a skirted, dual-sided settee in a large-scale floral pattern and mixed in upholstered pieces and sleek vintage furniture.

RIGHT The library is a snug retreat with walls, trim, and shelves swathed in a custom blue-tinted charcoal glaze that plays nicely with the vibrant, 11-color Pierre Frey rug.

ABOVE "What distinguished the three-story Queen Anne . . . was that it hadn't been destroyed in what I laughingly refer to as an 'awful renovation accident' during any of the decades since its late-19th-century heyday," muses Roberts.

RIGHT Roberts left the front facade of the home intact, removing the rear and adding a clean, spare kitchen and a family room, where quadrilateral forms are repeated in the limed-oak paneling, plush rug, and custom marble mantel.

ENGLISH GARDENS
EMERALD
VANITY FAIR PORTRAITS

LEFT Outfitted with original cabinetry, checkerboard-painted wood floors, and a vivid wallcovering by Tilton Fenwick for Duralee, the pantry is a showpiece in its own right. A chartreuse settee and a gold-framed portrait compose a captivating vignette.

ABOVE "The entertaining rooms were perfection," Roberts says. "All they needed was refurbishing the floors and stripping off years of paint to reveal the architectural beauty sleeping underneath." The dining room's blue dupioni silk curtains cascade toward a Louis XVI-style dining table.

LEFT The dining room walls are covered in a soft pink de Gournay wallpaper and rich mulberry-hued trim. A Louis XVI commode is framed by dining chairs in the same style.

"Old houses like this . . . need to be treated with reverence, despite it sometimes taking a bit more thought, effort, or money." —MARKHAM ROBERTS

LEFT A circa-1960 Carlo Nason for Mazzega pendant illuminates the stairwell. "The new paneling and stair in the central hall (leading to the basement) were designed to look original. But they don't feel old, because the paint treatment, wall upholstery, and contemporary art give the space a more vibrant feel," Roberts says.

RIGHT The primary bedroom suite addition features a soothing mix of undulating patterns in the Brunschwig & Fils' Le Touches wallpaper, the scalloped-edge bedding, and the voluminous curtains. The tufted, upholstered bed in an azure paisley and inviting chaise enhance the tranquil appeal.

COLONIAL COMEBACK

In Williamsburg, Virginia, designer Heather Chadduck Hillegas celebrates and elevates the storied patina of one of America's oldest homes.

PAGES 18-19 As the Williamsburg Designer in Residence, Hillegas had the singular experience of reimagining—and then residing in—the Nelson-Galt House, built around 1695. "I was working with a blank slate, more or less, with lots of stipulations given the historic easements." She swathed the parlor in a pale mural inspired by English "whitework" bed curtains.

ABOVE "The home's craftsmanship is astonishing," Hillegas says of the simple white frame dwelling, believed to be the oldest home in Colonial Williamsburg. It belonged to one family for some 200 years, and Thomas Nelson, one of its owners, was a signer of the Declaration of Independence.

RIGHT Hillegas envisioned the kitchen as a "handsome, masculine scullery to complement the rustic dining room." She applied blue-gray paint to the classic Shaker cabinets, topping them with local Virginia soapstone and installing brass hardware.

"These houses teach us so much about design."

—HEATHER CHADDUCK HILLEGAS

ABOVE "In the dining room, I wanted a moody, primitive feel, so I painted the ceiling blue and commissioned a crosshatch texture below the chair rail that brings the room to life," Hillegas says. The mural wallcovering is inspired by the work of English landscape designer Humphry Repton.

RIGHT Hillegas sees inspiration from Williamsburg in fashion today—"the way we dress beds, the trend toward patterned wallpapers and upholstery and wall murals that are so popular," she muses. Cornflower-blue pineapples and flowers bedeck the twin bedroom, which she trimmed in a woven silk gimp for a sweet finishing touch.

LEFT Hillegas chose fabrics that tell a story wherever she could. In the study, she wrapped the love seat in damask inspired by a 1750s silk gown that belonged to Martha Dandridge Custis Washington, "which she could well have worn here in Williamsburg, where her first husband had a townhouse and George often visited," says Hillegas.

RIGHT The Hepplewhite-style bed, with its elegant arched tester draped in a large-scale check, was made specifically for the deep green guest room.

SALADINO VILLA
RALPH LAUREN

LIVING LEGACY

Designer Philip Gorrivan reawakens a once-forgotten 1750s Colonial in the Connecticut countryside, restoring the historic residence to endure another 100 years.

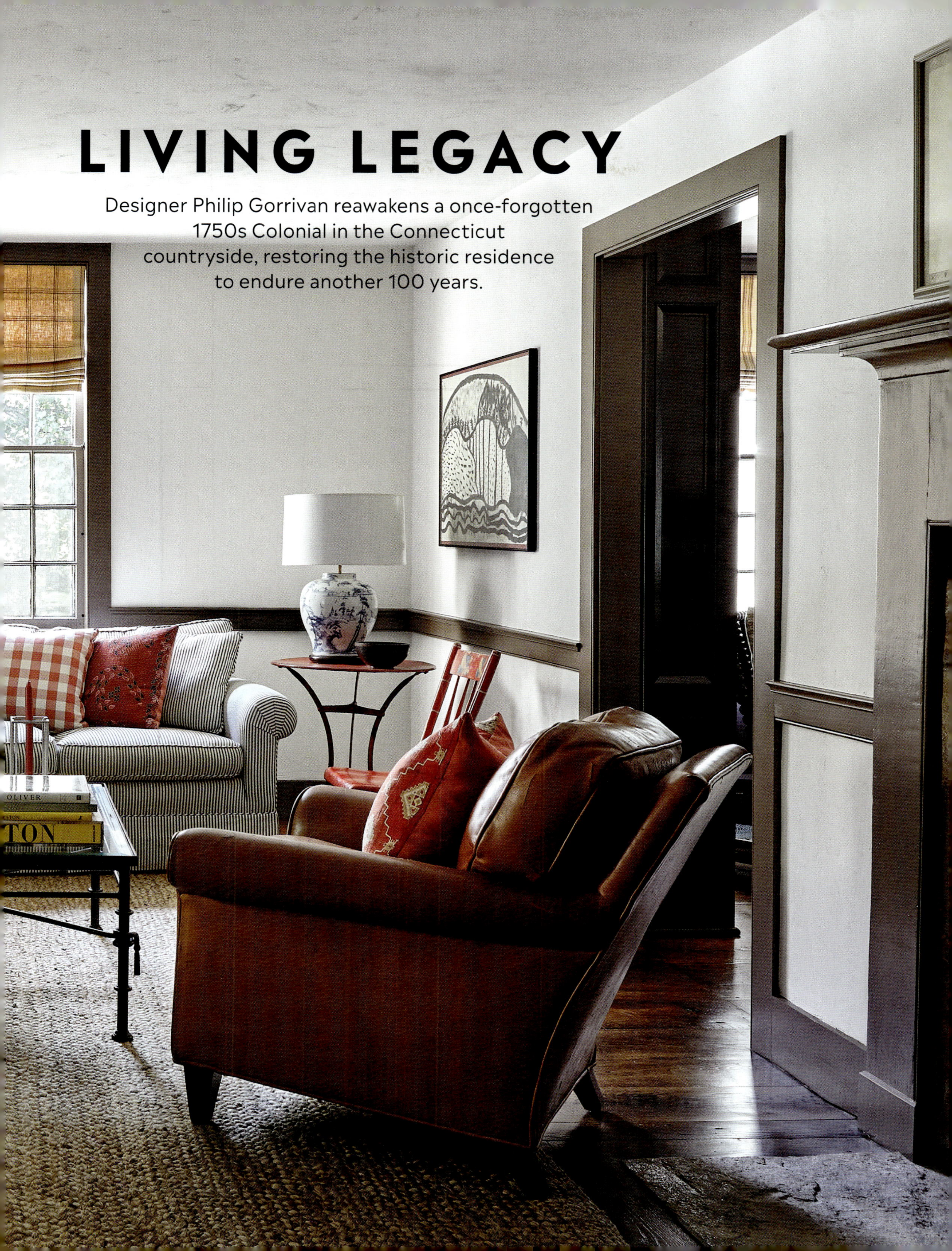

PAGES 24-25 In the two-story home in Washington, Connecticut, Gorrivan sought to preserve as many original details as he could. He refurbished wide-plank oak floors and rebuilt the fireplaces and chimney with original materials. In the easygoing living room, he installed antique French leather armchairs and a roll arm sectional in a vintage ticking stripe.

LEFT The entrance hall opens to wide oak flooring and an 18th-century stairwell. "It's a beautiful architectural element," he says.

ABOVE "I've always admired its symmetry and scale," Gorrivan says of the home's facade, with its side-gabled roof and central chimney, which was meticulously restored. "It is a perfect example of early American Colonial architecture."

LEFT While Gorrivan aimed to stay true to the home's period style, he took artistic license in some spaces, like the kitchen, where a Moroccan tile backsplash pops against maple butcher block and honed granite counters.

LES CONFITURES

PAGES 28-29 Gorrivan's dedicated research on Colonial New England architecture led him to add millwork throughout, from trim moldings around doors and windows to horizontal paneling, painted a warm gray in the breakfast room. The Gustavian-style buffet honors the homeowner's Swedish ancestry.

RIGHT Sunlight pours through a 1920s bay window illuminating a soaking tub and floral wallpaper by Josef Frank, a pioneer of Swedish modern design.

ABOVE Gorrivan devised a capacious new primary bedroom addition on the rear of the home, complete with details that add instant patina, like a beadboard tray ceiling and an ornately paneled Gustavian-style bed framed with built-in closets.

RIGHT Tributes to the homeowners' Swedish heritage abound, including a painted antique chest, a 19th-century Gustavian bed, and a 20th-century table lamp in a guest room. "The painted pieces, in particular, lighten and add a level of sophistication to this antique American house," Gorrivan says.

Peter Doig
AVEDON POWER
Jaime Parladé
A PERSONAL STYLE

CHAPTER 2

Room to Roam

Wide open spaces have always exerted a pull on the American psyche. Whether it's the freedom of movement our bodies crave, the access to nature in these undeveloped places, or a curiosity that pushes us to explore terrain in its natural state, the desire to have room of one's own seems to be in our blood.

It makes sense, then, that designers are attracted to out-of-town retreats, where creativity can wander and expand, too.

The homes in this collection, from a log cabin on 100 acres of Tennessee countryside to an 11,000-square-foot modern masterpiece with Rocky Mountain views for miles, inspire awe that matches the majesty of their settings.

In their beautiful and artful design they emphasize their connection to the land. Thoughtful choices—from the use of local stone and timber in ways that blur the lines between indoors and out, to walls of windows placed to highlight restorative vistas—enhance the sense of escape these houses provide.

This fluently coordinated dance between nature and comfort results in spaces that inspire resetting and reconnecting—with oneself, loved ones, the landscape, and the pace of the seasons.

Go ahead, take a deep breath and settle into the expanse.

◇◇◇

LEFT A custom mirror edged with shed antlers crowns the timber mantel in an Adirondack-style home in Sun Valley, Idaho, designed by Mark D. Sikes. Set on16 acres, the house has views of Idaho's Smoky Mountains, and unfettered access to incredible outdoor recreation is just outside.

ALPINE GLOW

Designer Mark D. Sikes tempers a Sun Valley, Idaho, cabin's "cowboy sensibility" with cozy colors, vibrant patterns, and touches of chinoiserie.

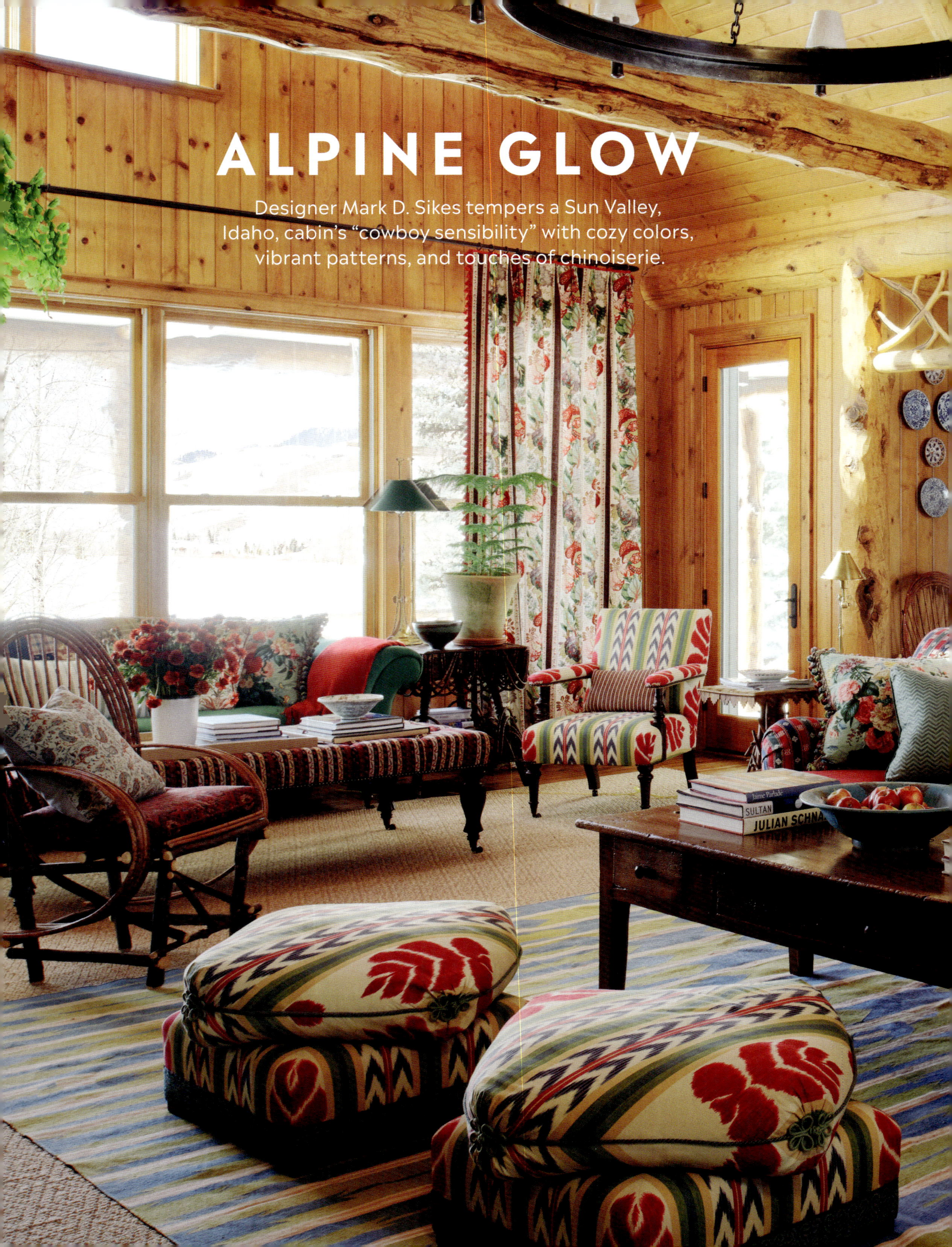

AVEDON POWER

PAGES 34-35 The living room's spirited mix of prints feels at home against the yellow pine paneling and bentwood details, which makes for an irresistibly inviting result. "Some people might be somewhat scared to layer all of this together, but these clients had no trepidation when it came to color and texture," Sikes says.

LEFT Sikes sprinkled blue-and-white decorative plates across paneled walls in the dining room, where ladderback chairs sport a duo of fabrics. Other designers interviewed by the homeowners suggested painting the walls in the home white, but Sikes advised against it. "Mark wanted to stay true to the original design and work off of this as a strength. He didn't view the style as something to fix," the homeowner says.

ABOVE Gray-green cabinetry mimics the tones of the landscape outside and complements the light-filled kitchen's soaring knotty-wood ceiling and delft tile backsplash. A brass-and-emerald range peeks out from behind the island, which is crowned with a two-tiered pot rack loaded with rustic charm.

LEFT A French folk art mirror and tapestry-inspired wallpaper depicting a woodland scene imbue a powder room with the coziness of a European chalet. Bright-blue trim caps the delft tiles.

BELOW A mélange of blossoms and soft pink patterns collide in this whimsical and warm bedroom, where the scalloped and skirted bed, fabric lampshades, and large ottoman give a sense of sweet femininity.

ABOVE In this seating area, Sikes employed natural materials—in the rattan chairs, seagrass wallcovering, and wooden furniture—as calm beats amid the eye-catching fabrics and decorative bookcase.

RIGHT The primary bedroom's variety of botanical motifs work in harmony thanks to complementary color palettes. "I think the magic of playing with so much texture and novelty is the repetition of things, whether it's using the same fabric in different places or linking pieces together with trim and other detailing," Sikes says.

VINEYARD HAVEN

Dan Fink reconnects a 1970s ranch to its Napa Valley setting with an airy floor plan, warm woodwork, and views that beckon toward olive trees, roses, wildflowers, and of course, grapevines.

PAGES 42-43 Architect Carl Baker of Ike Kligerman Barkley joined forces with Fink to infuse the home, located just outside of St. Helena, California, with modern soul. To expand the space, they crafted a great room addition with a lofty ceiling and bluestone floors. The hand-carved maple mantel is topped with an antique mirror framed by bluestone pilasters, and a pair of low-slung leather and glazed linen daybeds "can feel midcentury or Eastern," Fink says.

LEFT The kitchen feels both warm and quietly sophisticated, with cerused white oak cabinetry and bronze hardware. A quartet of sleek stools provide prime seating at the roomy island, which has slate-hued Brazilian soapstone counters.

RIGHT The subdued palette throughout the home is designed to let the half-acre property's views and natural light shine. Select chromatic splashes play up the beauty. For example, in the family room, the cinnabar-hued sofas and ottoman "evoke the magical golden hour there," says Fink.

KATSURA

"The owners wanted to break the mold of the quintessential wine country home and have a more modern feeling."

—DAN FINK

LEFT A new vineyard-facing screened porch, constructed where an awkward front portico once stood, is a favorite breakfast spot. Plantings of lavender and iceberg roses thrive before a grove of olive trees and grapevines beyond.

ABOVE Fink installed a Japanese-style wood soaking tub in the reconfigured primary bath, adding an earthy element to the sleek and modern space.

BIG SKY BEAUTY

A family escape designed by Suzanne Tucker at Montana's Yellowstone Club capitalizes on the open terrain of the American West with walls of glass and mountain-inspired materials.

PAGES 50-51 The new 11,000-square-foot home, designed by architect Reid Smith with interiors by Tucker, balances contemporary touches with rich, earthen hues and rugged materials organic to its 40-acre lot. The terrace, which can be enclosed, screened off, or left open, offers stunning vistas and a fireside perch for defrosting after a day on the slopes.

LEFT Walls in desert blonde sandstone from Utah emanate "beautiful russet, ochre, and coppery tones," says Tucker, as they rise toward the dining room's cedar-planked ceiling. A chandelier of glass fir tree ornaments twinkles above a walnut-and-hammered-iron table and box-woven chairs.

ABOVE "It's woods, it's stones, it's iron materials, it's skins and hides, but you take all of those elements and mix them up differently so that they come out in a more contemporary way," says Tucker of her modern take on Western style. In the family room, fresco-on-linen artwork commands attention above a custom sectional.

LEFT A radiant, russet-hued retreat with a charming set of built-in bunks is painted in Sienna Clay by Benjamin Moore. Drapery and textured rugs amp up the comfort and warmth.

LEFT In the primary bedroom, a linen banquette is front row to exquisite floor-to-ceiling views of snowcapped pines, firs, and miles of undulating terrain. The pale terra-cotta palette evokes the glow of a Rocky Mountain sunrise.

RIGHT The en suite primary bath is ensconced in onyx that features striations reminiscent of the walls of the Grand Canyon, Tucker says—they seem to radiate "this incredibly beautiful earthen quality."

STORYBOOK CABIN

Designers Brooke and Steve Giannetti transform a 175-year-old log home on 100 acres in Leiper's Fork, Tennessee, into a pastoral refuge centered on a deep kinship with nature, history, and community.

PAGES 56-57 Rusticity and elegance are entwined in the Giannettis' interiors business and their lovingly-restored farmstead and home, a circa 1850s log cabin they sought to make the "coziest possible place," Brooke says, "with nooks, rustic beams, and stonework."

LEFT A series of framed butterflies ties the dining room to the vibrant landscape outside. Antique seating—a Swedish sofa and Rococo chairs—surrounds the table, and an antique planter-turned-pendant illuminates meals.

ABOVE The kitchen creatively displays art from local Leiper's Creek Gallery. Open shelving contributes to the room's airiness, where stacks of sage-hued ceramics harmonize with the painted landscapes.

RIGHT To connect the living room more seamlessly with the garden, the couple enlarged the windows on either side of the fieldstone and antique barn beam fireplace. The space charms with its organic comfort, including a vintage leather sofa and antique stools.

ABOVE An antique Swedish table and Rococo stool from the Giannettis' store, Patina Home & Garden, set the stage for a sweet vignette of books, butterflies, and a trio of landscape paintings by Tennessee artist Meghan Aileen.

LEFT "There is a sense of story and history embedded in each piece," Brooke says of the assemblage of antiques that peppers their cabin. In the primary bedroom, an 18th-century Belgian verdure tapestry makes for a headboard, and a pair of carved reliefs flank the window.

VANITY FAIR 100 YEARS
JOHN DERIAN
RICHARD AVEDON EVIDENCE 1944–1994
AVEDON AN AUTOBIOGRAPHY

CHAPTER 3

American Glamour

Glamour can be bold, rich, and compelling. It can be lacquered walls, vibrant colors, sparkling metallics, and riveting patterns. Glamour is scene-stealing, personality-filled, and dazzling. But when it's done just right, glamour hinges on restraint and sophistication to maintain balance in a room. This is the challenge faced—and executed with aplomb—by the designers featured in the following pages: to craft a mix of indulgence and moderation for a result that is both dynamic and serene.

And while lavish interiors are nothing new—with roots that began to spread in the Art Deco movement of the Roaring '20s and the glitz of Hollywood Regency in the 1930s and beyond—today, glamour in America can assume many forms, as this chapter reveals. A Regency-style home in Richmond sports stunning custom millwork and ebullient florals. A resuscitated Art Deco abode in New Jersey is decked out in red lacquered ceilings and calming blue accents. In Dallas, just the right amount of gusto—in the form of ruffles, animal prints, and painted floors—achieves a midcentury Continental French look. On the coast of Maine, a summer house dials up the drama with wallpaper for days, and in Manhattan, over-the-top Americana overtakes a historic apartment with classic red, white, and blue and inviting large-scale furniture.

These spaces make a statement without shouting. They have fun without getting into trouble. Their designers knew when to get punchy and when to pull back, creating homes that feature moments of energy and calm. It's all about balancing the boldness.

◇◇◇

LEFT In a home in Richmond, Virginia, designer Suzanne Kasler delivers a lustrous emerald explosion of a library that matches the intensity of the home's striking spaces. Brass accents and a pair of mohair sofas are softened with a casual sea grass rug.

BEATON
LOUIS VUITTON
RICHARD AVEDON

HIGH IMPACT

A client's color palette parameters give designer Suzanne Kasler a thrilling challenge in a daringly chic Regency-style home in Richmond, Virginia.

PAGE 66 Aside from the punchy green library, the client wanted a limited colorway in her new home: a definitive selection of black, white, raspberry, and brown. In the family room, Kasler delivered glossy brown walls that mingle with a vivacious Casa Branca floral beneath an antique Venetian glass pagoda chandelier.

PAGE 67 A black-and-white checkerboard floor and delicately embellished iron-and-brass Paul Ferrante stools enliven the clean-lined kitchen.

ABOVE The front hall enfilade previews the home's courtyard-centric, rectangular O-shaped footprint, crafted by architectural designer Carter Skinner. A procession of antique armchairs upholstered in pink silk draws the eye across geometric black-and-white floors that echo the architectural forms.

RIGHT The two-toned, ink-and-ivory motif and pared-down use of pattern in the butler's pantry is akin to a palette cleanser among the home's more vibrant rooms. Large-scale floral artwork adds a graphic pop.

ABOVE De Gournay's Coco Coromandel wallpaper, inspired by the 17th-century Chinese lacquered screens Coco Chanel hung in her Paris apartment, lines the high-drama dining room. Through French doors, the room accesses the well-manicured courtyard. "When you have that classical balance with the landscape and architecture, it invites opportunities to push the envelope with design and color," says Kasler.

"The beauty of Regency style is that you can mix new and old very organically and you can layer in plenty of vintage pieces."

—SUZANNE KASLER

ABOVE Kasler's use of symmetry, subtle-yet-punchy graphics, and glamorous accents infuses the living room with quintessential Regency style and verve, with a leopard-print rug and an ornate interior scene shot by Massimo Listri.

RIGHT The primary bedroom balances serenity and sophistication, buoyed by the black-and-white chinoiserie wallpaper and curtains, the ebonized chest of drawers, and the canopy bed. The casual stripe of an inviting seating arrangement—a pattern that's repeated on the interior of the canopy bed's tailored curtains—offers a sense of ease.

BOLD & BRILLIANT

For a young family's home, designer Steven Gambrel infuses a once-stifled 1920s New Jersey estate with vibrant energy using lively patterns and intense colors.

PAGE 72 Gambrel worked in lockstep with architect Eric J. Smith to imbue the home with energy and vitality. "We wanted it to feel young and relevant," Gambrel says. A succession of elegant curves in the stairwell—in the arched window, tufted bench, and in Lourdes Sanchez's *Dots* (left)—are moderated by a series of framed color lithographs from Le Corbusier's *Le Poème de l'angle droit* (right).

PAGE 73 "The library and bar face the inner courtyard, so those spaces feel more nighttime, more rich," says Gambrel, who installed a vintage brass desk with commanding curves and selected dynamic, satin-brushed hues. "Wood paneling gives the library old-school resonance, while the youthfulness comes from the intense colors: teal, cinnabar lacquer."

ABOVE Gambrel covered dining room walls with gridded bark paper arranged to emulate the appearance of textured stone walls. A pair of lantern-style sconces, a natural fiber rug, and earth-going hues harmonize for a result that's organic, tactile, and welcoming.

RIGHT Smith transformed a former staff wing with upstairs bedrooms into a double-height kitchen with a row of clerestory windows. Gambrel added drama with a gunmetal-and-brass hood, an indigo-green marble island countertop, and golden leather cantilever seating.

LEFT "I love getting the furniture shapes to speak to each other, so you can be here as easily with two people as 20," Gambrel says of the living room's smart arrangement of intimate seating areas. Striéd walls and vintage lighting add to the effect.

RIGHT Smith devised a brand-new garden room to connect with a squash court turned guest wing. Gambrel placed a vintage baby grand piano, painted a chalky gray-beige, in one corner as a "really interesting and unexpected addition."

ABOVE Smith created a glassed-in conservatory from a portion of the original entry hall. Gambrel added potted orange trees, a quartet of custom chain-link mirrors, and apple-green upholstery for "a bite, like vinegar," he says.

HOUSE OF TREASURES

Designers Miles Redd and David Kaihoi outfit a 1930s Dallas home for a glittering third act.

PAGE 80 The homeowner, "a kind of Southern Coco Chanel," as described by Redd, desired color, layers, and "that particular high-style, 1930s-to-'60s Continental French look." In the dining room, the designers achieved this in part with silk tenting trimmed with a dashing indigo valance.

PAGE 81 The 1930s home had good bones but lacked drama. "You get the floors and walls right, and the rest is easy," Redd says. He and Kaihoi applied "cola"-colored lacquer to living room walls and grounded the space with an antique Qashqa'i rug.

LEFT The living room unfurls in a symphony of handblocked pastel flowers and sumptuous ruffles applied to plush sofas and armchairs with flourishes of animal prints and stripes. A gleaming Jean-Michel Frank–inspired coffee table was purchased at auction.

LEFT The kitchen is like an immersive art piece, with floors painted by Chris Pearson to imitate specimen marble and cabinets painted by Agustin Hurtado to resemble knotty blonde wood.

ABOVE The moss-green library is brimming with the homeowners' treasures, including an angular Venetian chandelier, a glossy Art Deco Macassar desk, and a pair of George II armchairs.

RIGHT The transportive family room is a visual feast, where a de Gournay Indian mural is studded with a George II carved pickled-pine mirror and paintings and drawings collected by the designers. A pair of doors upholstered in woven Madagascar cloth flank the Bridgewater-style sofa.

KINFOLK

BOLD MOVES

A quintessential Maine summer house puts on the glitz at the hands of designer Matthew Carter, with showstopping wallpaper, lacquered paneling, and checkerboard-painted floors.

PAGE 88 The "simple and lovely" summer escape was essentially move-in ready, but Carter's clients "wanted to vamp it up a bit," he says. In the guest room, he rolled out red accents—cherry lampshades, a scarlet coffee table, and a striped wool rug—against electric lime walls and a lush floral sofa.

PAGE 89 The entry hall, which Carter felt "wanted something maybe not so traditional," indulges with subtly stained checkerboard floors that meet statement-making star-patterned wallpaper—Miro by Albert Hadley, the design partner of Sister Parish, who summered nearby.

ABOVE "A deep color lets the walls recede and the windows expose the garden beyond," Carter says of the rich brown living room. Filled with pattern-clad vintage, custom seating, and alluring art, the room is "a grounding feature in the center of the house."

RIGHT The light and bright vaulted breakfast room is grounded with a striped green rug and a voluminous buffet. Rattan dining chairs and a wall of glass connect the porch and the water beyond.

MAINE HOUSE

LEFT “This space needed depth, it needed punch, it needed something more than just paint,” Carter says of the splashy study, where lacquered emerald paneling and bookcases gleam against custom green and ivory wallpaper.

ABOVE The dining room leans traditional with invigorating touches like vivid fern-print wallpaper bordered by a looping trim and softened with light blue ikat upholstery, a paper lantern pendant, and a thick woven rug.

RIGHT Burgeoning blooms—Albert Hadley's Beaton Rose wallpaper—flourish in the powder room. The simple wall-mount sink, vintage faucets, and decorative mirror boost the charm.

ABOVE The primary bedroom is a peaceful retreat. The walls are clad in a gingko print by Colefax and Fowler that mimics the verdant landscape along Maine's stunning coastline. The sage green armchair and ottoman invite further repose.

"There's so much design work that feels like it could be anywhere, but a home should nod to its place."

—MATTHEW CARTER

WEST SIDE STORY

Designer Anthony Baratta brings a fresh eye to the red, white, and blue panache of Americana style in an early-20th-century apartment in Manhattan.

PAGES 96-97 "I want you to walk in the door and say, 'Whoa,'" Baratta says of the historic Italian Renaissance apartment that he enveloped in attention-grabbing patterns and colors, like the exuberant living room's cherry-red velvet armchair and block-printed linen sofa.

ABOVE The entry hall's striped wallpaper and swagged border "has this luscious, tactile, handcrafted quality," Baratta says. An intricate American antique mirror hangs above an American Empire settee covered in ruby silk damask.

RIGHT "We used a scale of furniture that's meant for a space like this," says Baratta of the oversize rooms. "Sofas are big, chairs are high." In the custom-colored tartan study, an armchair is upholstered in an early American weaving-inspired print.

LOUIS VUITTON

LEFT In the kitchen, a theatrical window pelmet rises above what Baratta describes as a "1940s glam" banquette upholstered in diamond-patterned leather. Original mosaic tile floors inspire dove-gray cabinetry and trim.

ABOVE Cerise stripes adorn walls of the primary bedroom, where a pineapple finial bed designed by Baratta is decked in ethereal blue and punctuated at its foot with a curvaceous rouge Victorian recamier.

CHAPTER 4

By the Sea

Is there any deeper sigh than the one let out upon first entering a beach house? The ocean and the dwellings along it, no matter how humble or grand, proffer an inherent calm and sense of renewal that have attracted Americans to the shore for centuries. The sea captivates our senses, nudging each one to indulge—in the smell of salt in the air, the feel of weathered boardwalk planks beneath soles, the sound of sea foam sashaying ever closer to the dunes, the sight of the sun crossing the sky.

It's easy to heed the siren song of the sea—and the equally alluring homes that stud our shores. They call to us with the promise of settling into a slower rhythm ruled by the waves. The bounty of coastal living is profound in homes that speak fluently with the seascape and encourage gathering together away from the toil of the everyday to forge memories and connections that will sustain spirits for decades.

On Block Island, Rhode Island, a new shingle-style cottage with a charm that belies its large size sports a haute-pastoral spirit and small bedrooms that make space for the most important beach activity: convening with friends and family with easy access to the outdoors. In Nantucket, Massachusetts, a framed custom wallpaper panel by Gracie depicting the island lines up perfectly with the exterior horizon, and a palette of blue, yellow, and tawny golden brown evokes the sea, sun, and sand—the colors of a summer day. Near Charleston, South Carolina, cypress panels and sprawling windows relate to the Spanish moss-draped trees along the Kiawah River and beckon a young family to soak up the treasures of the low country.

◇◇◇

LEFT A new Block Island home sports views from the entrance straight through to the sea and boasts plenty of breezy gathering spaces inside and out where a family of six can savor the salty spoils of the coast.

NEW WAVE

Designer Miles Redd and architect Gil Schafer erect a chic, simple, and light-filled home on Block Island, with a renovated party barn-meets-poolhouse to boot.

LEFT A parade of botanicals draws the eye toward a custom-painted marble mirror, with ocean-inspired blues also surfacing in a pair of side chairs and the striking lacquer-and-brass pendant.

BELOW The library is a cozy reprieve with white oak paneling and a wall-to-wall sofa drenched in toile. A set of Billy Baldwin Studio slipper chairs with coordinating cushions invite conversation across a 19th-century Chinese camphorwood trunk given new life as a coffee table.

ABOVE Schafer plotted the spacious kitchen to enjoy "lots of light and views," including sight of a rare-to-the-island American elm tree, under the shade of which you can see nearly all the way to Montauk. A large metallic pendant crowns the pippy oak-topped island.

PAGES 104-105 The convivial living room's "blushy, pale pink" painted grasscloth walls were inspired by the floral linen, beloved by the homeowners, that covers the sofas and tufted armchairs. Redd applied skirts to the seating for an "old-fashioned, Sister Parishy" effect.

"The idea was just to have this beautiful, simple house that felt like it had been there forever."

—MILES REDD

ABOVE On the landing, *Waterfront* by Arthur Kimmel Getz, one of many marine-themed artworks, hangs over a seating nook between a collection of blue-and-white ceramics, creating a delightful pass-through or spot to rest a spell.

RIGHT Though the home is spacious at 5,300 square feet, the bedrooms are modestly sized. In a guest bedroom saturated in the Josef Frank-designed Citrus Garden wallpaper, bright blue and yellow weave together like the sun and sky around a rattan bed from Serena & Lily.

RIGHT "It was important to restore as much of it as possible," says Schafer of the barn, which he dismantled and rebuilt with reclaimed timber, adding a gable for an influx of sunlight. Today, the party-ready poolhouse boasts a bar, an expandable white oak dining table that can seat 20, and "the world's longest sofa," jokes Redd, where the family can gather to watch movies on a retractable screen.

ALLEGRA HICKS
YACHTS

HARBORSIDE HAVEN

A duo of historic townhouses on Nantucket's picturesque harbor are reconnected by designer Meg Braff into one airy, luminous vacation home.

PAGES 112–113 Braff and architect Gerard Beekman of New York–based Madison Worth Architecture brought two town home halves back together to create a sanctuary for a pair of empty nesters. In the sunlit family room, sleek swivel chairs and a cerused oak and lacquer coffee table gather beneath coffered ceilings with faux-bois wallcoverings that give the room "depth and make it feel so much higher," Braff says.

LEFT Sunny mornings are guaranteed in the cheerful breakfast room, where ochre walls are finished in a "rich and sophisticated textured plaster," Braff says. A light blue banquette and custom wicker chairs surround a table with fluted details.

ABOVE A duo of gold etageres, an antique raffia chair, and a white campaign desk coalesce amid rippling patterned wallpaper in the study, which has prime views of the water.

Heatherwick
NANTUCKET
NANTUCKET
VOGUE
TONY DUQUETTE
Leonardo

LEFT Fiery hues emanate from the library, with red and yellow seating across a vintage Maitland-Smith boat base coffee table. Vintage brass-and-lacquer bookcases by iconic designer Billy Baldwin, who summered on Nantucket and later retired there, and a metallic ceiling light enhance the glow.

LEFT The sweeping harbor-front deck is divided into a series of comfortable seating arrangements. The dining zone is shaded by a cheeky fringed canopy, and rattan chairs are topped with pale blue cushions.

RIGHT The primary bedroom opens to a stunning harborscape, with periwinkle walls that call to mind the sea at dusk. A punchy flower print peeks from the inside of the bed's canopy, and scalloped bedding from Leontine Linens supplements the softness.

"Our vision was expanded light, space, and connection."

—MEG BRAFF

LOWCOUNTRY GRANDEUR

A new home on James Island, South Carolina, is rooted in place, thanks to thoughtful connections to history and nature orchestrated by architect Stan Dixon and designer Tammy Connor.

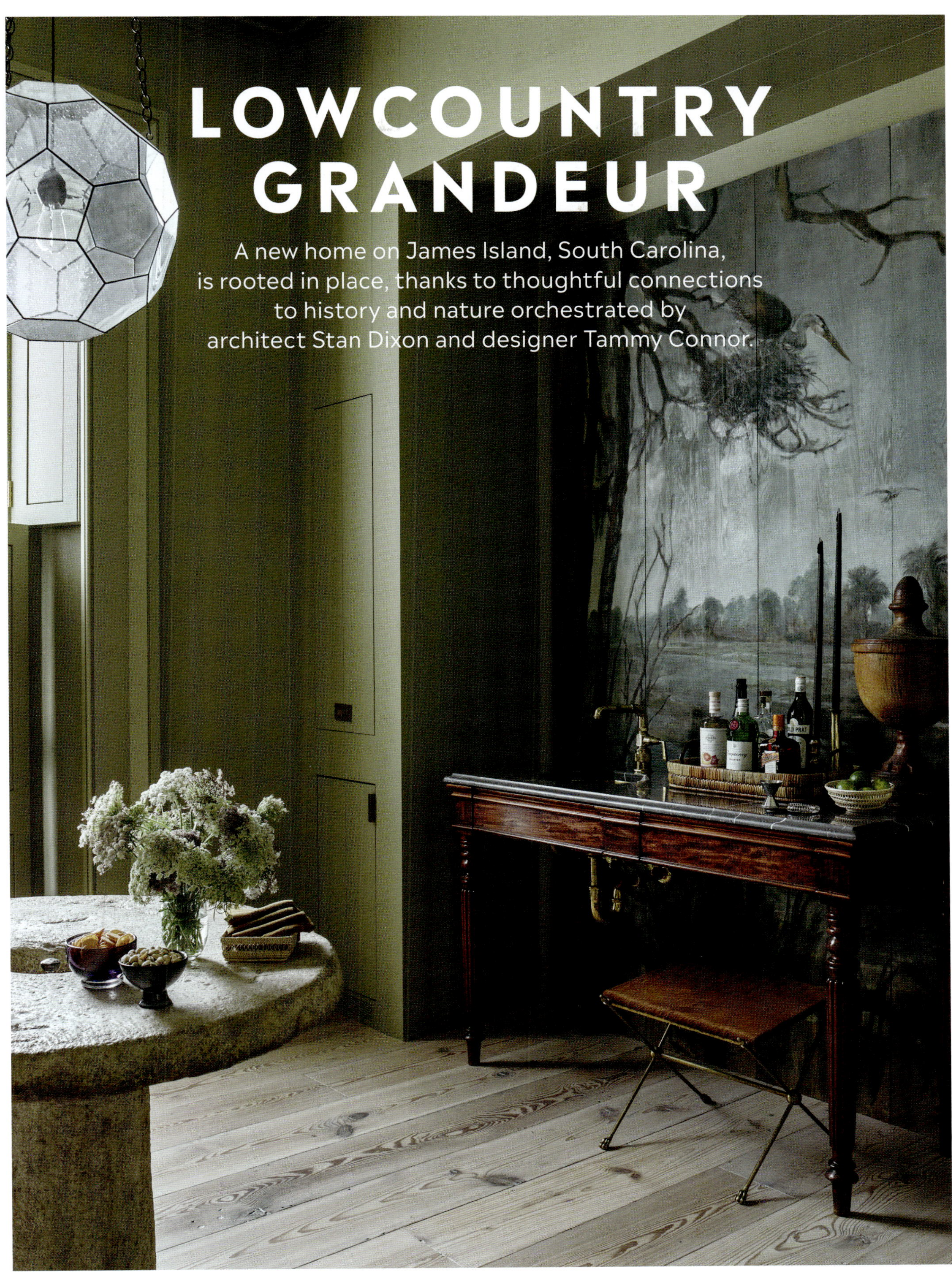

PAGE 120 With the house situated on a 27-acre parcel along the Kiawah River and surrounding marshlands, "much of what we did here was about connecting to the outside," says Dixon. In the breakfast room, French midcentury chairs pull up to a reclaimed pine farm-style table facing large-scale windows crafted of bronze.

PAGE 121 An English serving table turned bar off the entry celebrates the marsh landscape with a mural by Raymond Goins painted onto sinker cypress boards. Jib doors on either side keep bar appliances tucked away but within reach.

LEFT Artist Tyler Hays's harborfront painting on puzzle pieces hangs on cypress paneling in the library, where it informs the colors in the sapphire velvet English saddle-arm sofa and vibrant Art Nouveau patterned wing chair.

LEFT A captivating constellation of ceramic blooms by sculptor Bradley Sabin festoons a grass cloth-covered enclave, transforming the stair landing into an absorbing sitting area. A shagreen-wrapped coffee table by Michael Morrow adds textural and angular intrigue.

LEFT Painted brick walls and 12-inch-wide heart pine planked flooring in a swept finish impart age to the kitchen, important for homeowners who wanted their new home to have a strong sense of history. Etched glass pendants glow above a wood-topped island and rattan-and-rawhide stools.

RIGHT The primary bedroom's nuanced color palette is subdued but striking with a tonal arrowroot wallcovering balanced with abstract art. A lacquered Parsons-style nightstand and upholstered headboard complete the look.

CHAPTER 5

New Traditions

A riff on convention or an updated classic is like a balm, the perfect mix of old and new that reaches across eras to impart comfort and intrigue. Take an antique dresser topped with abstract art or a cozy wood-paneled family room crowned with a modern pendant light, for example. This pleasing cross-pollination of time periods embodies a spirit that feels uniquely American, simultaneously embracing a groundedness in history and excitement for the future.

Capturing the best of traditional design and imbuing it with contemporary touches is a hallmark of the homes in this chapter.

American designers are reimagining the classics, whether by restoring older homes to fit busy lifestyles while honoring the past or crafting a sense of history in a new build that will become the setting for traditions to come. These spaces revel in legacy without succumbing to stuffiness, and they embrace modern conveniences without being cold. Mastering this juxtaposition is design craft, and you'll find a wealth of inspiration here.

From a light-filled new home in California laden with antiques and warm pattern to a clapboard Colonial in Dallas wrapped in earthy textiles and punctuated with killer pop art, to a freshly constructed Chicago manse that forgoes a formal living room in favor of a laid-back family room and an incredible two-story library, these homes are clear classics that also charm with the perfect sprinkle of refreshing whimsy.

◇◇◇

LEFT Designer Peter Dunham's trademark mix of vivid prints, milk-paint-clad walls, and natural materials coalesce in a convivial pink-and-blue moment in a Newport, California, home. A pair of cotton Indian dhurries cover the floor and daybed.

ROOM TO GROW

A family's fresh start on their old Newport Beach, California, lot is aged to perfection by the vintage-hunting genius of designer Peter Dunham.

PAGE 128 Architect Bob White of Forest Studio "choreographed everything based on the lot" when designing a new space for an avid gardener and her husband. A bluestone patio off the family room features a built-in dining banquette outfitted in stripes and fig leaves from Dunham's fabric line.

PAGE 129 "You want to lead with the strongest element, right?" says Dunham of the views of roses, nasturtium, citrus, and olives afforded through the family room's purposefully undressed windows. The designer's ingenuity with found objects is on display here—he transformed French leather wrestling mats into an oversize ottoman.

ABOVE Cavalier King Charles spaniels luxuriate in the new poolhouse, designed in the style of English countryside cottages. A collection of 19th-century Persian tiles are set into plaster walls in custom Indian blue milk paint.

RIGHT "I tell my clients early on that I'm likely to call saying I'd found such and such, and they have to buy it," jokes Dunham. In the case of the library, it was "the holy grail of architectural salvage"—50 feet of 18th-century brass wire-front bookcases found at auction in England and tailored to fit the library. Dunham cut down the legs of a Georgian sideboard for a desk that is broad enough to fit the window nook.

LEFT A steel-and-brass custom hood inspired by 19th-century English homes crowns the kitchen, planned to a T with the wife, who is a passionate cook. Sage clay tiles and rush-backed stools add texture, grounding the predominantly white space.

ABOVE Nasturtium wallpaper, a nod to the garden outside, climbs the office walls, culminating in a fantastic leafy green light fixture found at auction. Trim and built-ins are painted a fittingly verdant hue.

Henry
HAIR
DONALD
Andy Warhol
REFLECTION
lisa perry

BOHEMIAN SPIRIT

An elegant clapboard Colonial in Dallas is the perfect foil to its pop artist owner and his family, thanks to designer Cathy Kincaid's mix of sophisticated taste with a sense of humor.

LEFT For pop art icon Donald Robertson and his wife, Kimberly Gieske, a move to Texas necessitated combining their divergent tastes—his, a bit chaotic, hers, more orderly—within the confines of a traditional home. Enter Kincaid, who crafted an abode with a "collected, casual, educated look at things" that suits them both. The living room fireplace is topped with a spirited floral painting by Michael de Feo flanked with single-arm sconces.

LEFT A patterned taupe linen wallcovering from Namay Samay and curtains in an allover avian motif create a graphic backdrop for a stocky white lacquered table and 18th-century-style chairs in the dining room. A tasseled rope chandelier adds a touch of whimsy.

ABOVE Kincaid, who has a penchant for textiles and obtaining fabrics from lesser-known sources, cloaked utilitarian pendants in slipcovers fashioned from French linen tea towels in the kitchen. Creatively displayed art and artifacts pop against green-gray cabinets and paneling.

PAGES 134-135 In the family room, Robertson's artwork—mixed with pieces by sons Henry (far left) and Charlie (near right)—pops amid tailored upholstery, white trim, and a wool rug in tidy stripes that harnesses hues from around the room.

"The house looks very buttoned up, but if you look closely, there's still some nonsense going on."

—ARTIST AND HOMEOWNER DONALD ROBERTSON

ABOVE Throughout the house, as here in the living room, the kids' artwork graces the walls, intermixed here with an array of vintage seascapes.

RIGHT "I collect art from new dads," Donaldson says in his tongue-and-cheek fashion, "because I know they're all probably desperate for cash." In one of his son's rooms, a chromatic abstract painting by artist Sebo Walker contrasts with Sister Parish wallpaper and a traditional English faux-bamboo chest found at Round Top.

BAD BLOOD
PATHFINDERS SOCIETY
NERDS

WINDY CITY WONDERLAND

Designer Summer Thornton marries bold formality with cozy hospitality for a Chicago home that brims with color, pattern, softness, and a touch of grandeur.

THE SUN KING
VICTORIA
A.N. WILSON
GREAT CATHERINE
CECIL BEATON
AMERICANS IN PARIS
FOUR LIVES IN PARIS
THE PEACEMAKERS
JOHN GRISHAM
E.M. FORSTER
A LIFE
P.N. FURBANK
PICASSO & MAYA

PAGES 140-141 A carpet of blooms in the form of a late-18th-century Ukrainian needlepoint rug grounds the family room, where an eclectic mix of patterns—stripes, block-print botanicals, and the knotty wood of the pine walls—plays host to lively gatherings around an ebony-finished oak coffee table.

LEFT One study hosts an inspired assemblage of pastels. Pink plaid walls in the style of Gloria Vanderbilt's 1972 Southampton bedroom mingle with hand-painted trim, an homage to a design from the Bloomsbury group's 1910s English farmhouse.

ABOVE The homeowner's desire for a two-story library inspired them to build a new home, designed by architect Heidi Lightner. Nearly 2,000 books line the shelves of the hand-cerused European white oak-paneled space, which features hand-turned banisters, a custom-crafted colored-glass laylight, and richly colored furnishings, including an orange mohair velvet sofa edged in bouillon and fringe and plum-leather chairs.

"The husband is quite formal and bold, the wife more casual and cozy, so we wanted to create this grand shell and then interject color, pattern, and softness."

—SUMMER THORNTON

ABOVE Chicago's punishing winters did not deter the homeowners from creating spaces that bridge indoors and out. A breakfast conservatory gets a playful twist with decorative black-and-honey rattan chairs and "peanut-butter-and-jelly" zellige floor tiles.

LEFT The receiving room is dripping with chic storage inside glossy green cabinetry fronted with cane inserts. The ceiling's berry and flower trellis wallpaper is a charming and unexpected finish.

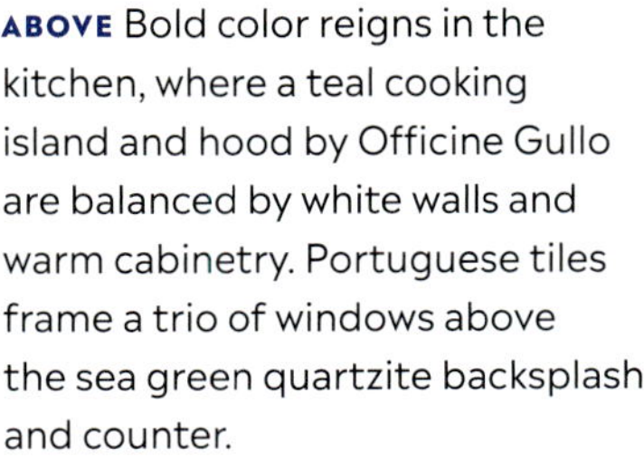

ABOVE Bold color reigns in the kitchen, where a teal cooking island and hood by Officine Gullo are balanced by white walls and warm cabinetry. Portuguese tiles frame a trio of windows above the sea green quartzite backsplash and counter.

LEFT A sitting room is a wow moment, with olive-green lacquered walls, a skirted banquet topped with throw pillows in two colorways of a Décors Barbares floral, and a blood orange mohair chair. A 1960s Salvador Dalí lithograph and repeating sconces dress up walls.

ABOVE A sea of pattern—blue and green stripes, ochre checks, and rambling 18th-century-inspired floral vines—engulfs a guest bedroom for a one-of-a-kind escape. A decorative side table and scrolling trim above add an elegant effect to the recessed bed.

CHAPTER 6

Modern Visions

Clean lines, natural materials, open spaces, neutral palettes, bold details, and a deep connection and deference to the landscape—this is modern style in America, a country of dreamers raised to look ahead and imagine what could be. This optimism and desire to harness our ingenuity, resilience, and capacity for progress while honing our vision for the future holds a deep kinship with the revolutionary spirit of contemporary style.

If, when you envision a modern home, you imagine stark, space-age motifs that prize technology and austerity over connection, allow today's arbiters of design to deftly demonstrate that modern interiors are some of the warmest, most invigorating spaces you'll encounter. These homes are simple, elegant and forward-thinking with a keen eye for comfort, rejuvenation, and harmony between indoors and out.

From a chic Dallas manse decked out in ebony accents to a modernist, window-clad North Carolina lake house that blends seamlessly into the mountainside, and a Los Angeles light-filled farmhouse enriched with a museum-worthy art collection, these homes open the door to a fresh approach to modern design. Welcome to the future—and the dawn of the next 250 years of American design.

◇◇◇

LEFT Curving walls, contrasting vertical and horizontal paneling, and vibrant artwork launch the high-drama entry of designers David and Ann Sutherland's modernist Dallas home.

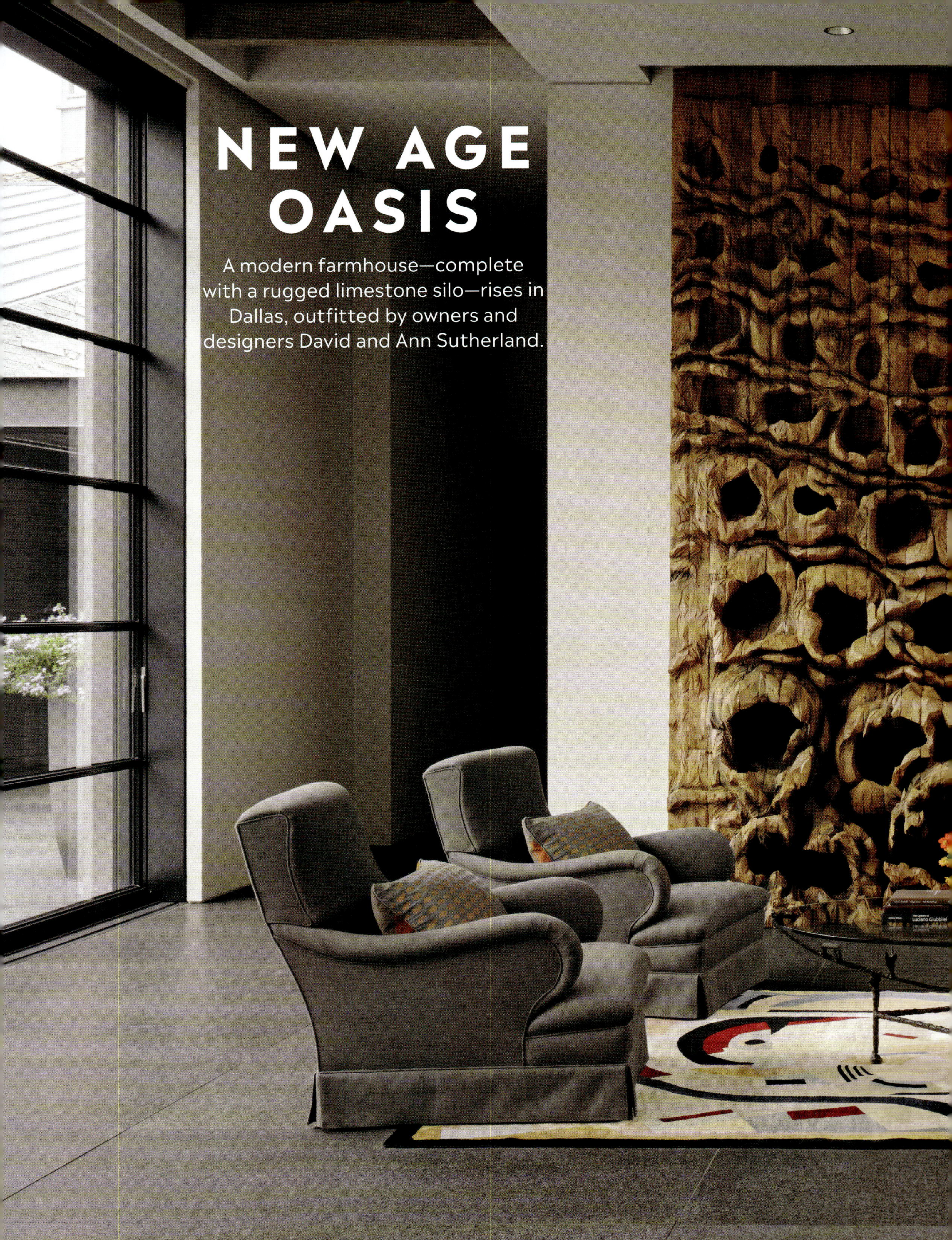

NEW AGE OASIS

A modern farmhouse—complete with a rugged limestone silo—rises in Dallas, outfitted by owners and designers David and Ann Sutherland.

LEFT A steel stairway ascends the limestone silo, spiraling skyward to access a top-floor guest suite. An antique sculpture stands within the curving structure.

BELOW In the kitchen, a trio of teak stools with brushed stainless steel accents sidle up to the silver-and-white island below an altar-inspired light fixture. The black backsplash echoes the kitchen's granite floors. "We don't use a lot of color, and black was definitely a thematic shade for us—I find it so chic," says Ann Sutherland.

ABOVE A custom table, with a sculptural bronze base and leather parchment top finished in polyurethane, is like artwork in the dining room. The homeowners' arrangement of furnishings creates negative space that highlights their collection of paintings and sculptures.

PAGES 150-151 The homeowners, founders of Sutherland Furniture and Perennials Fabrics, collaborated with modernist architect Lionel Morrison to create a contemporary dream home. An ascendant cedar sculpture by Ursula von Rydingsvard stretches past the living room ceiling into a niche designed just to house the piece.

"Art should always evoke an emotion, whether positive or negative." –DAVID SUTHERLAND

ABOVE The second-floor guest suite is wrapped in soothing neutrals and a wealth of texture. The designers applied a lime-based paint that "has a smooth and luminous value to it that looks like stone," Ann says. A black-and-white painting by Richard Giglio punctuates the space.

RIGHT The breakfast room's soaring steel window and skylight reinforce the importance of the home's relationship to the two-and-a-half-acre property, dotted with live oaks and inviting terraces. Linear patterns in the rug, artwork by Santiago Parra, and shadows cast from the windows and beamed ceiling add interest and movement.

RUSCHA
de Kooning
HARING
DESIGN

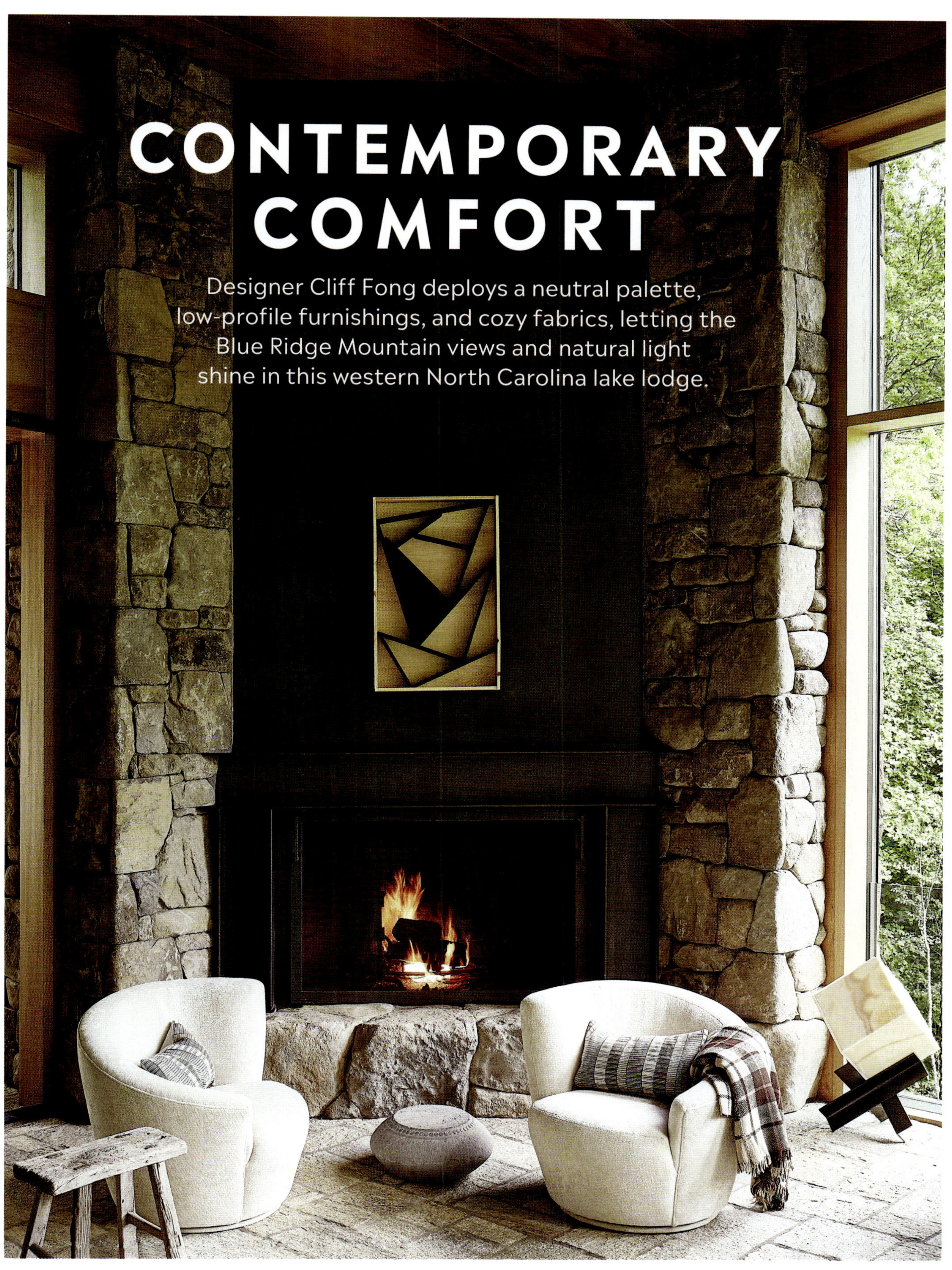

CONTEMPORARY COMFORT

Designer Cliff Fong deploys a neutral palette, low-profile furnishings, and cozy fabrics, letting the Blue Ridge Mountain views and natural light shine in this western North Carolina lake lodge.

PAGE 156 The Lake Toxaway home, designed by architects Al and Parker Platt, features a great room that boasts no shortage of fun, from the custom pool table beneath a Dante drum chandelier to the secret bookcase bar, hidden behind a mechanical panel topped with contemporary artwork by Alexander Calder.

PAGE 157 The covered terrace, accessible from the dining room, sports a duo of vintage Vladimir Kagan swivels, which can rotate to face the hearth or the wooded hillside that rolls toward the lake. An angular piece by Japanese artist Nobuo Sekine accentuates the height and organic atmosphere of the sitting area.

LEFT Materials with history and regional connection outfit the lodge. The dining table and chairs, below a vintage Poul Henningsen artichoke pendant, are made of reclaimed wood and leather, and the fireplace is constructed of local Fines Creek granite.

ABOVE A custom-hued kitchen island with Juno limestone, also used for the backsplash and behind shelving, sits among cabinetry commissioned by Fong in the style of midcentury woodworker George Nakashima.

LEFT Retractable screens on the covered flagstone terrace enhance the home's relationship with the five-acre parcel, which is dotted with pine, oak, sourwood, and black gum trees, as well as gardens, lawns, paths, and a small beach by the water.

ABOVE Enthusiastic entertainers, the homeowners built a separate house for visiting friends and family. In this guest room, an upholstered Italian bed set against preweathered ipe-paneled walls is an inviting place to recharge.

MATISSE
IN THE BARNES FOUNDATION
Federico
Fellini

STATE OF THE ART

A Los Angeles residence designed by Michael S. Smith is guided by the homeowners' stellar collection of paintings and sculptures and relationship to the outdoor rooms of the three-acre property.

LALANNE
LOTUSLAND
WAYS of DRAWING
INTERIORITIES
YAYOI KUSAMA
BASQUIAT

PAGES 162-163 Quiet solids and neutral prints swath generous sofas, armchairs, and a chaise, enveloping the living room in enticing softness. English painter Hurvin Anderson's *Country Club* and the expansive windows draw the outside in.

LEFT Designed by architect Howard Backen, a pioneer of the modern farmhouse movement, the great room evokes an upscale barn, with bleached walnut planks and a wall of glass that all but disappears for unimpeded access to a multitude of outdoor rooms.

ABOVE The kitchen's sleek, restrained design grants top billing to Kenneth Noland's *Mexican Camino*, which stretches above the backsplash like a vibrant range hood. A duo of pendants by French artist Philippe Anthonioz appear as hanging sculptures.

LEFT Smith describes the house as being "almost woven throughout the garden, with unexpected points of union between the two." *Déméter*, a marble sculpture by Jean Arp, seems to beckon visitors into the garden from the sunlit hall.

LEFT In the husband's study, striations of blue in the sofa, daybed, and rug guide the eye toward David Hockney's *Paper Pool: Diving Board*, created with Tyler Graphics. A three-tiered Pagani Studio chandelier illuminates the space.

RIGHT A vintage wool rug by textile artist Ingrid Hellman-Knafve in shades of earth and sky unifies the sunroom and the three-acre grounds, as does the faux-bois table base, woven sofa, and footed tables and chairs.

"The house and the garden blend so well to provide moments for reflection and appreciation of nature."

—MICHAEL S. SMITH

LEFT The city of Los Angeles peeks through an open window beyond the soaking tub in the wife's bathroom. A bronze chandelier by Claude Lalanne features a kaleidoscope of butterflies perched on branches.

LEFT Shearling-covered armchairs invite repose beneath a pool scene by Hurvin Anderson, which electrifies the blonde walnut paneled walls and peaceful color scheme in the primary bedroom. Metal accents in the bedside dressers and textured bronze ottoman add warmth and intrigue.

INDEX

NOTE: Page references of photos indicate locations of captions.

◇◇◇

A

Adirondack-style home, 33. *See also* Sun Valley cabin
Aileen, Meghan, 60
Americana apartment. *See* Manhattan Americana apartment
American glamour. *See* Glamorous homes
Anderson, Hurvin, 165, 169
Anthonioz, Philippe, 165
Apartment. *See* Manhattan Americana apartment
Architects
- Backen, Howard, 165 (*See also* Los Angeles modern farmhouse)
- Baker, Carl, 45 (*See also* Napa Valley ranch)
- Beekman, Gerard, 115 (*See also* Nantucket harborside house)
- Dixon, Stan, 121 (*See also* James Island riverfront house)
- Lightner, Heidi, 143 (*See also* Chicago whimsical home)
- Morrison, Lionel, 153 (*See also* Dallas new-age farmhouse)
- Platt, Al and Parker, 159 (*See also* Blue Ridge Mountain lake lodge)
- Schafer, Gil, 105, 107, 110 (*See also* Block Island beach house)
- Skinner, Carter, 68 (*See also* Richmond Regency-style home)
- Smith, Eric J., 74 (*See also* New Jersey Art Deco abode)
- Smith, Reid, 53 (*See also* Yellowstone family retreat)
- White, Bob, 130 (*See also* Newport Beach update)

Arp, Jean, 167
Art Deco home. *See* New Jersey Art Deco abode
Art Deco Macassar desk, 85
Art Nouveau furniture, 123

B

Backen, Howard, 165. *See also* Los Angeles modern farmhouse
Baker, Carl, 45. *See also* Napa Valley ranch
Balcony, 118
Baldwin, Billy, 106, 117
Bar, 74, 123, 156, 159
Baratta, Anthony, 96–101. *See also* Manhattan Americana apartment
Bathroom
- Los Angeles modern farmhouse, 169
- Maine summer house, 94
- Napa Valley ranch, 49
- Sun Valley cabin, 38
- Washington historic Colonial, 30
- Yellowstone family retreat, 55

Beach house. *See* Seaside houses
Beaton Rose wallpaper, 94
Bedroom (bunkroom), 55
Bedroom (child's), 138
Bedroom (feminine), 38
Bedroom (guest)
- Block Island beach house, 108
- Blue Ridge Mountain lake lodge, 161
- Chicago whimsical home, 147
- Dallas new-age farmhouse, 154
- Maine summer house, 90
- Washington historic Colonial, 30
- Williamsburg historic Colonial cottage, 23

Bedroom (primary)
- Greenwich historic Queen Anne, 16
- James Island riverfront house, 125
- Leiper's Fork log home, 63
- Los Angeles modern farmhouse, 169
- Maine summer house, 95
- Manhattan Americana apartment, 101
- Nantucket harborside house, 118
- Richmond Regency-style home, 70
- Sun Valley cabin, 40
- Washington historic Colonial, 30
- Yellowstone family retreat, 55

Bedroom (twin), 22
Beekman, Gerard, 115. *See also* Nantucket harborside house
Big Sky family escape. *See* Yellowstone family retreat
Billy Baldwin Studio, 106, 117
Block Island beach house, 103, 104–111
- bedroom, 108
- exterior, 103
- kitchen, 107
- landing, 108
- library, 106
- living room, 106, 107
- passageway, 108
- pool house, 110
- sitting area, 106
- stairway, 108
- views, 103, 107, 110

Bloomsbury group, 143
Blue Ridge Mountain lake lodge, 156–161
- bar, 156, 159
- bedroom (guest), 161
- dining room, 159
- exterior, 159, 161
- fireplace, 159
- great room, 159
- guest house, 161
- kitchen, 159
- terrace, 159, 161
- views, 159, 161

Braff, Meg, 112–119. *See also* Nantucket harborside house
Breakfast room
- Chicago whimsical home, 145
- Dallas new-age farmhouse, 154
- James Island riverfront house, 123
- Maine summer house, 90
- Nantucket harborside house, 115
- Washington historic Colonial, 30

Brunschwig & Fils wallpaper, 16
Butler's pantry, 68

Cabin. *See* Sun Valley cabin
Calder, Alexander, 159
California. *See* Napa Valley ranch; Newport Beach update
Carter, Matthew, 88–95. *See also* Maine summer house

Casa Branca floral fabric, 68
Chicago whimsical home, 140–147
  bedroom, 147
  breakfast conservatory, 145
  family room, 143
  kitchen, 145
  library, 143
  receiving room, 145
  sitting room, 147
  study, 143
  views, 145
Citrus Garden wallpaper, 108
Classic homes reimagined. *See* New traditions
Coco Coromandel wallpaper, 68
Colefax and Fowler, 95
Colonials. *See* Dallas bohemian Colonial; Washington historic Colonial; Williamsburg historic Colonial cottage
Connecticut. *See* Greenwich historic Queen Anne; Washington historic Colonial
Connor, Tammy, 120–125. *See also* James Island riverfront house
Conservatory, 78, 145
Contemporary updates of traditional design. *See* New traditions
Continental French house. *See* Dallas Continental French home
Cottages. *See* Williamsburg historic Colonial cottage
Country Club (Anderson), 165

D

Dalí, Salvador, 147
Dallas bohemian Colonial, 134–139
  bedroom, 138
  dining room, 137
  family room, 137
  fireplace, 136
  kitchen, 137
  living room, 136, 138
Dallas Continental French home, 80–87
  dining room, 83
  family room, 86
  kitchen, 85
  library, 85
  living room, 83
Dallas new-age farmhouse, 149, 150–155
  bedroom, 154
  breakfast room, 154
  dining room, 153
  entry, 149
  exterior, 154
  kitchen, 152
  living room, 153
  stairway, 152
  views, 154
Dante lighting, 159
Deck, 118
Décors Barbares, 146
De Gournay mural, 86
De Gournay wallpaper, 15, 69
Déméter (Arp), 167
Designers
  Baratta, Anthony, 96–101 (*See also* Manhattan Americana apartment)
  Braff, Meg, 112–119 (*See also* Nantucket harborside house)
  Carter, Matthew, 88–95 (*See also* Maine summer house)
  Connor, Tammy, 120–125 (*See also* James Island riverfront house)
  Dunham, Peter, 127, 128–133 (*See also* Newport Beach update)
  Fink, Dan, 42–49 (*See also* Napa Valley ranch)
  Fong, Cliff, 156–161 (*See also* Blue Ridge Mountain lake lodge)
  Gambrel, Steven, 72–79 (*See also* New Jersey Art Deco abode)
  Giannetti, Brooke and Steve, 56–63 (*See also* Leiper's Fork log home)
  Gorrivan, Philip, 24–31 (*See also* Washington historic Colonial)
  Hillegas, Heather Chadduck, 9, 18–23 (*See also* Williamsburg historic Colonial cottage)
  Kaihoi, David, 80–87 (*See also* Dallas Continental French home)
  Kasler, Suzanne, 65, 66–71 (*See also* Richmond Regency-style home)
  Kincaid, Cathy, 134–139 (*See also* Dallas bohemian Colonial)
  Redd, Miles, 80–87, 104–111 (*See also* Block Island beach house; Dallas Continental French home)
  Roberts, Markham, 9, 10–17 (*See also* Greenwich historic Queen Anne)
  Sikes, Mark D., 33, 34–41 (*See also* Sun Valley cabin)
  Smith, Michael S., 162–169 (*See also* Los Angeles modern farmhouse)
  Sutherland, Ann and David, 149, 150–155 (*See also* Dallas new-age farmhouse)
  Thorton, Summer, 140–147 (*See also* Chicago whimsical home)
  Tucker, Suzanne, 50–55 (*See also* Yellowstone family retreat)
Dining room
  Blue Ridge Mountain lake lodge, 159
  Dallas bohemian Colonial, 137
  Dallas Continental French home, 83
  Dallas new-age farmhouse, 153
  Greenwich historic Queen Anne, 15
  Leiper's Fork log home, 59
  Maine summer house, 94
  New Jersey Art Deco abode, 74
  Richmond Regency-style home, 69
  Sun Valley cabin, 37
  Williamsburg historic Colonial cottage, 21
  Yellowstone family retreat, 53
Dixon, Stan, 121. *See also* James Island riverfront house
Dots (Sanchez), 74
Dunham, Peter, 127, 128–133. *See also* Newport Beach update
Duralee, 15

E

Early-20th-century apartment. *See* Manhattan Americana apartment
Early American Colonial architecture. *See* Washington historic Colonial; Williamsburg historic Colonial cottage
English Aesthetic Movement furniture, 9
Entry and entrance hall
  Dallas new-age farmhouse, 149
  James Island riverfront house, 123
  Maine summer house, 90
  Manhattan Americana apartment, 98
  Richmond Regency-style home, 68
  Washington historic Colonial, 27
Expansive spaces. *See* Out-of-town retreats
Exterior
  Block Island beach house, 103
  Blue Ridge Mountain lake lodge, 159, 161
  Dallas new-age farmhouse, 154
  Greenwich historic Queen Anne, 12
  Los Angeles modern farmhouse, 167, 169
  Napa Valley ranch, 49
  Washington historic Colonial, 27
  Williamsburg historic Colonial cottage, 20

F

Family retreat. *See* Yellowstone family retreat
Family room
  Chicago whimsical home, 143
  Dallas bohemian Colonial, 137

(Family room, continued)
Dallas Continental French home, 86
Greenwich historic Queen Anne, 12
Leiper's Fork log home, 59
Nantucket harborside house, 115
Napa Valley ranch, 46
Newport Beach update, 127
Richmond Regency-style home, 68
Yellowstone family retreat, 53
Farmhouses. *See* Dallas new-age farmhouse; Leiper's Fork log home; Los Angeles modern farmhouse
Fenwick, Tilton, 15
Ferrante, Paul, 68
Fink, Dan, 42–49. *See also* Napa Valley ranch
Fong, Cliff, 156–161. *See also* Blue Ridge Mountain lake lodge
Frank, Jean-Michel, 83
Frank, Josef, 30, 108
French folk art mirror, 38
Frey, Pierre, 12

G

Gambrel, Steven, 72–79. *See also* New Jersey Art Deco abode
Garden room, 78
Georgian furniture, 9, 85, 86, 130
Getz, Arthur Kimmel, 108
Giannetti, Brooke and Steve, 56–63. *See also* Leiper's Fork log home
Gieske, Kimberly, 136
Giglio, Richard, 154
Glamorous homes, 64–101
about, 65
Americana apartment in New York, 96–101 (*See also* Manhattan Americana apartment)
Art Deco abode in New Jersey, 72–79 (*See also* New Jersey Art Deco abode)
Continental French home in Texas, 80–87 (*See also* Dallas Continental French home)
Regency-style home in Virginia, 65, 66–71 (*See also* Richmond Regency-style home)
summer house in Maine, 88–95 (*See also* Maine summer house)
Goins, Raymond, 123
Gorrivan, Philip, 24–31. *See also* Washington historic Colonial
Great room, 45, 159, 165
Greenwich historic Queen Anne, 9, 10–17
addition, 12
bedroom, 16
dining room, 15
exterior, 12
family room, 12
kitchen, 12, 15
landing, 9, 16
library, 12
living room, 12
stairway, 9, 16
Guest house, 161
Gustavian-style furniture, 30

H

Hadley, Albert, 90, 94
Halls and passageways, 108, 167
Harborside house. *See* Nantucket harborside house
Hays, Tyler, 123
Hellman-Knafve, Ingrid, 167
Henningsen, Poul, 159
Hepplewhite-style bed, 23
Hillegas, Heather Chadduck, 9, 18–23. *See also* Williamsburg historic colonial cottage
Historic homes, 9–31
about, 9
Colonial cottage in Virginia, 9, 18–23 (*See also* Williamsburg historic Colonial cottage)
Colonial in Connecticut, 24–31 (*See also* Washington historic Colonial)
Queen Anne in Connecticut, 9, 10–17 (*See also* Greenwich historic Queen Anne)
Hockney, David, 167
Hurtado, Agustin, 85

I

Ike Kligerman Barkley (firm), 45
Illinois. *See* Chicago whimsical home
Italian Renaissance apartment. *See* Manhattan Americana apartment

J

James Island riverfront house, 120–125
bar, 123
bedroom, 125
breakfast room, 123
entry, 123
kitchen, 125
landing, 125
library, 123
views, 123

K

Kagan, Vladimir, 153, 159
Kaihoi, David, 80–87. *See also* Dallas Continental French home
Kasler, Suzanne, 65, 66–71. *See also* Regency-style home
Kiawah River. *See* James Island riverfront house
Kincaid, Cathy, 134–139. *See also* Dallas bohemian Colonial
Kitchen
Block Island beach house, 107
Blue Ridge Mountain lake lodge, 159
Chicago whimsical home, 145
Dallas bohemian Colonial, 137
Dallas Continental French home, 85
Dallas new-age farmhouse, 152
Greenwich historic Queen Anne, 12, 15
James Island riverfront house, 125
Leiper's Fork log home, 59
Los Angeles modern farmhouse, 165
Manhattan Americana apartment, 101
Napa Valley ranch, 45
New Jersey Art Deco abode, 74
Newport Beach update, 133
Richmond Regency-style home, 68
Sun Valley cabin, 37
Washington historic Colonial, 27
Williamsburg historic Colonial cottage, 20

L

Lake Toxaway. *See* Blue Ridge Mountain lake lodge
Lalanne, Claude, 169
Landing, 9, 16, 108, 125. *See also* Stairway
Le Corbusier, 74
Leiper's Creek Gallery, 59
Leiper's Fork log home, 56–63
bedroom, 63
dining room, 59
family room, 59
kitchen, 59
living room, 60
stairway, 60
views, 57, 59, 60
Leontine Linens, 118
Le Poème de l'angle droit (Le Corbusier), 74
Le Touches wallpaper, 16
Library
Block Island beach house, 106
Chicago whimsical home, 143

Dallas Continental French home, 85
Greenwich historic Queen Anne, 12
James Island riverfront house, 123
Nantucket harborside house, 117
New Jersey Art Deco abode, 74
Newport Beach update, 130
Richmond Regency-style home, 65
Lightner, Heidi, 143. *See also* Chicago whimsical home
Listri, Massimo, 70
Living room
Block Island beach house, 106, 107
Dallas bohemian Colonial, 136, 138
Dallas Continental French home, 83
Dallas new-age farmhouse, 153
Greenwich historic Queen Anne, 12
Leiper's Fork log home, 60
Los Angeles modern farmhouse, 165
Maine summer house, 90
Manhattan Americana apartment, 98
New Jersey Art Deco abode, 77
Newport Beach update, 130
Richmond Regency-style home, 70
Sun Valley cabin, 37
Washington historic Colonial, 27
Log cabin. *See* Leiper's Fork log home
Los Angeles modern farmhouse, 162–169
bathroom, 169
bedroom, 169
exterior, 167, 169
great room, 165
hall, 167
kitchen, 165
living room, 165
study, 167
sunroom, 167
views, 165, 167, 169
Lowcountry home. *See* James Island riverfront house

M

Maine summer house, 88–95
bathroom, 94
bedrooms, 90, 95
breakfast room, 90
dining room, 94
entry hall, 90
living room, 90
study, 93
views, 90
Maitland-Smith coffee table, 117
Manhattan Americana apartment, 96–101
bedroom, 101
entry hall, 98
kitchen, 101
living room, 98
study, 98
Massachusetts. *See* Nantucket harborside house
Mexican Camino (Noland), 165
Miro wallpaper, 90
Modern farmhouse movement, 165
Modern homes, 149–169
about, 149
farmhouse in California, 162–169 (*See also* Los Angeles modern farmhouse)
lake lodge in North Carolina, 156–161 (*See also* Blue Ridge Mountain lake lodge)
new-age farmhouse in Texas, 149, 150–155 (*See also* Dallas new-age farmhouse)
Montana. *See* Yellowstone family retreat
Morrison, Lionel, 153. *See also* Dallas new-age farmhouse
Morrow, Michael, 125

N

Nakashima, George, 159
Namay Samay, 137
Nantucket harborside house, 112–119
balcony, 118
bedroom, 118
breakfast room, 115
deck, 118
family room, 115
library, 117
outdoor dining, 118
study, 115
views, 115, 118
Napa Valley ranch, 42–49
bathroom, 49
exterior, 49
family room, 46
great room addition, 45
kitchen, 45
screened porch, 49
views, 46, 49
Nature-inspired homes. *See* Out-of-town retreats
Nelson-Galt House, 20. *See also* Williamsburg historic Colonial cottage
New-age farmhouse in Texas. *See* Dallas new-age farmhouse
New Jersey Art Deco abode, 72–79
bar, 74
conservatory, 78
dining room, 74
garden room, 78
kitchen, 74
library, 74
living room, 77
stairway, 74
Newport Beach update, 127, 128–133
family room, 127
kitchen, 133
library, 130
living room, 130
office, 133
patio, 130
pool house, 130
sitting room, 127
views, 130
New traditions, 126–147
about, 127
bohemian-style in Texas, 134–139 (*See also* Dallas bohemian Colonial)
update in California, 127, 128–133 (*See also* Newport Beach update)
whimsical home in Illinois, 140–147 (*See also* Chicago whimsical home)
New York City. *See* Manhattan Americana apartment
Noland, Kenneth, 165
North Carolina. *See* Blue Ridge Mountain lake lodge

O

Officine Gullo, 145
Outdoor spaces
Block Island beach house, 110
Blue Ridge Mountain lake lodge, 159, 161
Los Angeles modern farmhouse, 165, 167
Nantucket harborside house, 118
Napa Valley ranch, 49
Newport Beach update, 130
Yellowstone family retreat, 53
Out-of-town retreats, 32–63
about, 33
cabin in Idaho, 33, 34–41 (*See also* Sun Valley cabin)
family retreat in Montana, 50–55 (*See also* Yellowstone family retreat)
log home in Tennessee, 56–63 (*See also* Leiper's Fork log home)
ranch in California, 42–49 (*See also* Napa Valley ranch)

P

Pagani Studio, 167
Paper Pool: Diving Board (Hockney), 167
Parish, Sister, 9, 90, 107, 138
Parlor, 20
Parra, Santiago, 154
Parsons-style furniture, 125
Passageways and halls, 108, 167
Patina Home & Garden, 60
Patio, 130
Pearson, Chris, 85
Perennials Fabrics, 153
Platt, Al and Parker, 159. *See also* Blue Ridge Mountain lake lodge
Pool house, 110, 130
Pop-artist's home. *See* Dallas bohemian Colonial

Q

Qashqa'i rug, 83
Queen Anne. *See* Greenwich historic Queen Anne

R

Ranch. *See* Napa Valley ranch
Rattan furniture, 39, 90, 108, 118, 125, 145
Receiving room, 145
Redd, Miles, 80-87, 104-111. *See also* Block Island beach house; Dallas Continental French home
Regency-style home. *See* Richmond Regency-style home
Repton, Humphry, 21
Rhode Island. *See* Block Island beach house
Richmond Regency-style home, 65, 66-71
- bedroom, 70
- butler's pantry, 68
- dining room, 69
- family room, 68
- front hall, 68
- kitchen, 68
- library, 65
- living room, 70

Riverfront house. *See* James Island riverfront house
Roberts, Markham, 9, 10-17. *See also* Greenwich historic Queen Anne
Robertson, Donald, 136, 137, 138
Rocky Mountains. *See* Yellowstone family retreat
Rococo chairs, 59
Room to roam. *See* Out-of-town retreats
Round Top, 138

S

Sabin, Bradly, 125
Sanchez, Lourdes, 74
Schafer, Gil, 105, 107, 110. *See also* Block Island beach house
Screened porch, 49
Seaside houses, 102-125
- about, 103
- beach house in Rhode Island, 103, 104-111 (*See also* Block Island beach house)
- harborside house in Massachusetts, 112-119 (*See also* Nantucket harborside house)
- riverfront home in South Carolina, 120-125 (*See also* James Island riverfront house)

Serena & Lily, 108
Sikes, Mark D., 33, 34-41. *See also* Sun Valley cabin
Sister Parish wallpaper, 138
Sitting room, 39, 106, 127, 147
Skinner, Carter, 68. *See also* Richmond Regency-style home
Smith, Eric J., 74. *See also* New Jersey Art Deco abode
Smith, Michael S., 162-169. *See also* Los Angeles modern farmhouse
Smith, Reid, 53. *See also* Yellowstone family retreat
Smoky Mountains (Idaho), 33. *See also* Sun Valley cabin
South Carolina. *See* James Island riverfront house
Stairway. *See also* Landing
- Block Island beach house, 108
- Dallas new-age farmhouse, 152
- Greenwich historic Queen Anne, 9, 16
- Leiper's Fork log home, 60
- New Jersey Art Deco abode, 74
- Washington historic Colonial, 27

St. Helena, California, 45. *See also* Napa Valley ranch
Storybook cabin. *See* Leiper's Fork log home
Study
- Chicago whimsical home, 143
- Los Angeles modern farmhouse, 167
- Maine summer house, 93
- Manhattan Americana apartment, 98
- Nantucket harborside house, 115
- Williamsburg historic Colonial cottage, 22

Summer house. *See* Maine summer house
Sunroom, 167
Sun Valley cabin, 33, 34-41
- bathroom, 38
- bedrooms, 38, 40
- dining room, 37
- kitchen, 37
- living room, 37
- seating area, 39
- views, 33

Sutherland, Ann and David, 149, 150-155. *See also* Dallas new-age farmhouse
Sutherland Furniture, 153
Swedish design, 30, 59, 60

T

Tennessee. *See* Leiper's Fork log home
Terrace, 53, 159, 161
Texas. *See* Dallas bohemian Colonial; Dallas Continental French home; Dallas new-age farmhouse
Thorton, Summer, 140-147. *See also* Chicago whimsical home
Townhouse. *See* Nantucket harborside house
Traditional design with contemporary updates. *See* New traditions
Tucker, Suzanne, 50-55. *See also* Yellowstone family retreat
Tyler Graphics, 167

Vanderbilt, Gloria, 143
Vervoordt, Axel, 153
Victorian revival. *See* Greenwich historic Queen Anne; Washington historic Colonial; Williamsburg historic Colonial cottage
Vineyard ranch in California. *See* Napa Valley ranch
Virginia. *See* Richmond Regency-style home; Williamsburg historic Colonial cottage
Von Rydingsvard, Ursula, 153

Walker, Sebo, 138
Washington, Martha Dandridge Custis, 22
Washington historic Colonial, 24-31
- bathroom, 30
- bedrooms, 30
- breakfast room, 30
- entrance hall, 27

exterior, 27
kitchen, 27
living room, 27
stairway, 27
Waterfront (Getz), 108
Western style. *See* Yellowstone family retreat
West Side apartment. *See* Manhattan Americana apartment
White, Bob, 130. *See also* Newport Beach update
Williamsburg historic Colonial cottage, 9, 18–23
bedrooms, 22, 23
design inspiration from, 9
dining room, 21
exterior, 20
history, 20
kitchen, 20
parlor, 20
study, 22

Yellowstone family retreat, 50–55
bathroom, 55
bedrooms, 55
dining room, 53
family room, 53
fireplace, 53
terrace, 53
views, 53, 55

PHOTOGRAPHY CREDITS

Eric Piasecki cover (Artwork on left: Christopher Martin, *Loro I*, 2018, acrylic on acrylic, 48 x 36 inches), 72–79, 102, 104–111, 120–125, back cover
Noe Dewitt 1, 80–87
Annie Schlechter 2–3, 18–23, 112–119
Max Kim-Bee 4, 32, 34–41
Thomas Loof 6, 140–147
Nelson Hancock 8, 10–17
Joshua Mchugh 24–31
Roger Davies 42–49, 50–55
Lisa Romerein 56–63
Melanie Acevedo 64, 66–71
Erin Little 88–95
Mark Roskams 96–101
David Tsay 126, 128–133
Douglas Friedman 134–139, 148, 150–155
William Abranowicz 156–161
Michael Mundy 162–169
Brian Woodcock 175 (bottom)

SUSAN HALL MAHON is a lifestyle journalist and editor covering home, garden, food, health, and travel. She got her start at *Southern Living* magazine after graduating with a journalism degree from the University of North Carolina at Chapel Hill and has held top editorial roles at *Allrecipes.com*, *Coastal Living*, *Myrecipes.com*, and *Health* magazine. She lives in Birmingham, Alabama, where she loves to hike and play outside with her husband, two young daughters, and senior citizen hound dog.

STEELE THOMAS MARCOUX is the editor of VERANDA and a veteran of the design publishing industry, having served in senior editorial roles at *Country Living, Coastal Living,* and *Southern Living*. She is a member of the board of directors of the Alabama School of Fine Arts in Birmingham, where she lives with her husband, two sons, and two dogs.

EDITOR IN CHIEF Steele Thomas Marcoux
CREATIVE DIRECTOR Victor Maze
EXECUTIVE EDITOR Ellen McGauley
MANAGING EDITOR Amy Lowe Mitchell
VISUAL DIRECTOR Kate Phillips
VISUAL EDITOR Ian Palmer

HEARST HOME
VICE PRESIDENT, PUBLISHER, HEARST BOOKS Jacqueline Deval
DEPUTY MANAGING EDITOR, HEARST BOOKS Maria Ramroop
SENIOR PHOTO EDITOR Cinzia Reale-Castello

AUTHOR Susan Hall Mahon
PROJECT EDITOR Leah Tracosas Jenness
ART DIRECTOR & DESIGNER Erynn Hassinger
DIGITAL IMAGE SPECIALIST Ruth Vazquez
COPY EDITOR Vanessa Weiman

PUBLISHED BY HEARST
PRESIDENT & CHIEF EXECUTIVE OFFICER Steven R. Swartz
CHAIRMAN William R. Hearst III
EXECUTIVE VICE CHAIRMAN Frank A. Bennack, Jr.

HEARST MAGAZINE MEDIA INC
PRESIDENT Debi Chirichella
GENERAL MANAGER, HEARST HEARST FASHION & LUXURY GROUP Alicianne Rand
GLOBAL CHIEF REVENUE OFFICER Lisa Ryan Howard
EDITORIAL DIRECTOR Lucy Kaylin
CHIEF FINANCIAL & STRATEGY OFFICER; TREASURER Regina Buckley
CONSUMER GROWTH OFFICER Lindsey Horrigan
CHIEF PRODUCT & TECHNOLOGY OFFICER Daniel Bernard
PRESIDENT, HEARST MAGAZINES INTERNATIONAL Jonathan Wright
SECRETARY Catherine A. Bostron
PUBLISHING CONSULTANT Mark F. Miller

Library of Congress Cataloging-in-Publication Data available on request

10 9 8 7 6 5 4 3 2 1

Published by Hearst Home, an imprint of Hearst Books/Hearst Communications, Inc.
300 W 57th Street New York, NY 10019

For information about custom editions, special sales, premium and corporate purchases hearst.com/magazines/hearst-books

Printed in China
978-1-958395-62-2